DATE DUE

GAYLORD			PRINTED IN U.S.A.

PEOPLE OF THE
GREAT BASIN

by
LINDA THOMPSON

Rourke
Publishing LLC
Vero Beach, Florida 32964

www.rourkepublishing.com

PHOTO CREDITS:
Library of Congress, Prints & Photographs Division, Edward S. Curtis Collection: cover, title page, pages 14, 15, 21, 27, 29, 33, 35, 36, 42; Andreas Trawny: page 4; Courtesy of The Division of Anthropology, American Museum of Natural History (AMNH): pages 5, 8, 12, 13, 19, 22-25, 35, 38, 39, 42, 43; Courtesy of the National Anthropological Archives, Smithsonian Institution Museum: pages 6, 9, 15, 26, 32, 36, 37, 39, 40; Cindy Hegger: page 8; Library of Congress, Buckaroos in Paradise Collection: pages 9, 28, 30, 42, 43; Denver Public Library: page 10; Charles Reasoner: pages 13, 19; U.S. Fish & Wildlife Service: page 18.

DESIGN AND LAYOUT by Rohm Padilla, Mi Casa Publications, printing@taosnet.com

Library of Congress Cataloging-In-Publication Data

Thompson, Linda, 1941-
  People of the Great Basin / by Linda Thompson.
      p. cm. -- (Native peoples, Native lands)
Includes bibliographical references and index.
Contents: The Great Basin people today -- Where they came from -- Life in the Great Basin -- What they believe.
  ISBN 1-58952-754-2 (hardcover)
  1. Indians of North America--Great Basin--History--Juvenile literature. 2. Indians of North America--Great Basin--Social life and customs--Juvenile literature. [1. Indians of North America--Great Basin.] I. Title. II. Series: Thompson, Linda, 1941-   Native peoples, Native lands.
  E78.G67T45 2003
  979.004'97--dc21
                                            2003011534

Printed in the USA

TITLE PAGE IMAGE:
Fishing with a gaff-hook - Paviotso man; photo by Edward S. Curtis

TABLE OF CONTENTS

Point Rock, Utah

Chapter I:

PEOPLE OF THE GREAT BASIN

*T*he **Great Basin People** descended from the survivors of more than a dozen **Native American** (or **American Indian**) tribes. They once inhabited a vast region that now includes parts of nine states. Today's Great Basin People mostly live on **reservations** in Nevada, Colorado, Utah, Wyoming, Idaho, and eastern California.

The Great Basin is a region of mountains, rivers, and high meadows. The land is at least 5,000 feet (1,524 m) above sea level. Mountains are high, with an average of 10,000 feet (3,048 m). Rivers do not drain toward any ocean because of mountain ranges in all directions. For that reason, water drains into **sinkholes** that tend to be salty. One large sinkhole is Utah's Great Salt Lake.

Great Salt Lake, Utah
photo by Andreas Trawny

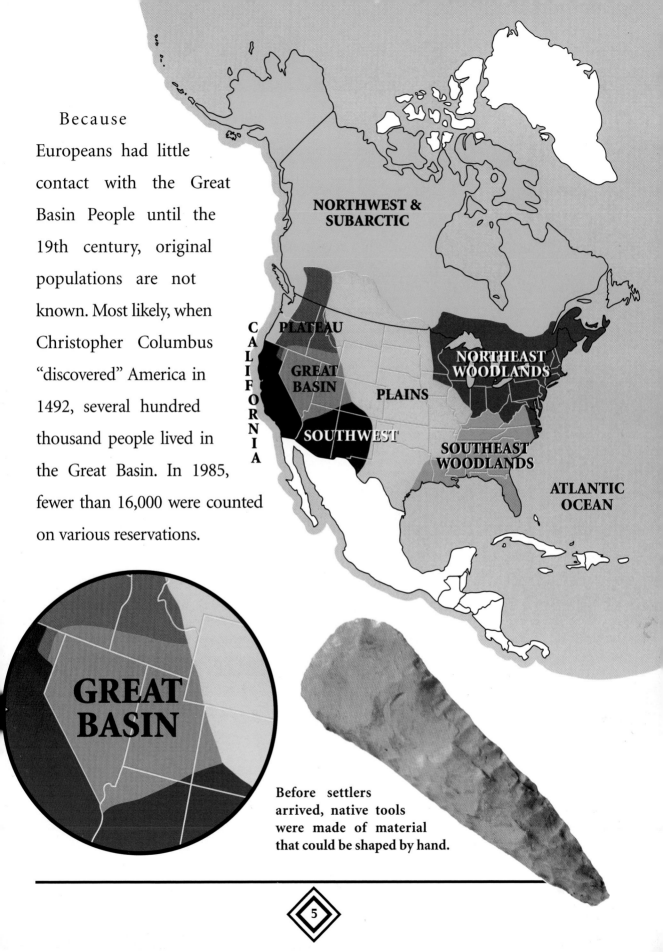

Because Europeans had little contact with the Great Basin People until the 19th century, original populations are not known. Most likely, when Christopher Columbus "discovered" America in 1492, several hundred thousand people lived in the Great Basin. In 1985, fewer than 16,000 were counted on various reservations.

NORTHWEST & SUBARCTIC

PLATEAU

C A L I F O R N I A

GREAT BASIN

PLAINS

SOUTHWEST

NORTHEAST WOODLANDS

SOUTHEAST WOODLANDS

ATLANTIC OCEAN

GREAT BASIN

Before settlers arrived, native tools were made of material that could be shaped by hand.

This coin featuring Sacagawea was issued by the U.S. Mint

Sacagawea [Sah-cah' gah-we-ah], or "Bird Woman," is the most famous Shoshone. Born to the Lemhi Shoshone, she was kidnapped at age 11 by the Hidatsa. They sold her to a French-Canadian fur trader. In November 1804, the **Lewis and Clark Expedition** asked her to be their guide. With her husband and baby, Sacagawea accompanied the expedition to the Pacific Ocean. A valuable guide and interpreter, she also showed the men how to find edible plants. After the trip, Sacagawea returned to the Hidatsa.

The land's high salt content and climate make the Great Basin one of the most difficult natural places for people to live. The climate is **semiarid** and has extremes of heat and cold. There is scant natural plant life, mostly sagebrush and grasses. This region supports fewer animals than many other parts of the United States. To survive, Great Basin People learned to eat even such things as gophers, lizards, and grasshoppers. Most of their time was spent searching for food. Therefore, they had a more primitive lifestyle than other Native groups.

The early Great Basin People did no farming. They lived in bands of perhaps 50 to 200 individuals, scattered throughout a huge area. They spoke many languages that came from **Shoshonean**, now called **Uto-Aztecan**. It has very old roots in **Aztec**, the language of central Mexico. The main groups speaking Uto-Aztecan were the Shoshone, the Paiute, and the Ute. Also, smaller groups such as the Washoe on the eastern flanks of California's Sierra Nevada Mountains spoke an unrelated language.

Rock arch in the painted desert in Utah

From as early as 1600, Great Basin People began to encounter Europeans. In 1637, Spaniards who had settled in New Mexico captured a group of Utah, or Ute, People and forced them into slavery. In the 17th century, the Ute sometimes joined the Spanish in fighting other Natives, such as the Comanche. After they got horses, the Ute began participating in raids against Spanish and Indian villages from New Mexico to Kansas. By the middle of the 1800s, these and other Great Basin People had begun to trade with Europeans and their American descendants.

War hammer made of wood with a stone tied on using sinew

War ax with metal head shows influence of settlers on native weaponry.

Mormon missionary, baptizing Natives at the Virgin River in 1875

The first major European impact on tribes of the Basin came from the **Mormons**, a religious group. They settled near the Great Salt Lake in 1847. Also, with the California Gold Rush of 1849 and the discovery of rich silver deposits in Nevada in 1859, thousands of people heading west crossed the Basin. Some of them stayed, becoming ranchers and farmers.

In 1869, a large railroad was completed, spanning the continent. This brought more and more settlers into the Great Basin. They chose the most desirable sites to live, near water. Their cattle ranged widely, ruining the sparse vegetation that supported game animals and people. In general, the Army protected the claims of the newcomers against those of Natives.

Natives on mountaintop watching a train

Ute camp at the Garden of the Gods in 1913

Everywhere in the New World, Natives lost their land bit by bit and had to give up the relationship they enjoyed with nature. Through **treaties** with U.S. and territorial governments, the Great Basin People surrendered their lands in exchange for something else. Often the "something else" turned out to be much less than they had been promised.

In this region, it did not help that Natives frequently were at war with each other. Great Basin tribes such as the Ute and Shoshone were under constant threat from Plains People on the north and east. Europeans gave Natives guns and ammunition to defend themselves against raiding tribes such as the Crow, Blackfeet, Sioux, Cheyenne, and Arapaho. Therefore, Great Basin peoples tended to side with Europeans in conflicts with Plains tribes. For instance, the Eastern Shoshone protected travelers along the **Oregon Trail**. This was a major route for settlers moving to the Northwest.

As Europeans and their descendants pressed west, they urged their government to open up more land for settlement. The U.S. Government persuaded Great Basin leaders to sign treaties that created reservations. Some leaders disagreed with the terms of these treaties, and only a few would sign them. Still, the government made the treaties apply to everyone.

Thousands of Great Basin descendants have merged into the general population, but many still live on reservations. Although the sizes and shapes of reservations have changed over the years, one thing is generally true. Each U.S. reservation has its own government with a **sovereign nation** status. This means that people living there have their own laws and tribal organizations, and in many ways are not subject to U.S. or state laws. For example, reservations have created gambling **casinos** in states where gambling is otherwise illegal. The casinos create jobs and provide money for schools and other programs to raise the standard of living.

These days, Great Basin People live in houses, drive cars, watch television, and eat many of the same foods that other Americans eat. Children go to public schools and their parents work at a variety of jobs. But to maintain the family cooperation and closeness they once had, families still come together for **powwows** and rodeos, and they try to take time off from jobs and schools to attend these gatherings.

Wherever they live, Native peoples are actively engaged in preserving their heritage. For example, they still make traditional baskets and other items. Some tribes continue to practice their tribal languages, songs, dances, and ceremonies and teach them to younger generations. They understand that by engaging in these things, they can keep their history and values alive.

Traditional Wolf Dance outfit

Through singing, dancing, and **drumming**, the Great Basin People continue to tell their stories. Although their lives will never be what they once were, together they have managed to keep their traditions alive. These tribes have also produced a number of individuals who have achieved recognition in art, music, film, writing, teaching, and other fields. By listening to their voices, Natives and non-Natives alike can better understand who the Great Basin People were and still are.

Adrian C. Louis, Lovelock Paiute, is a leading Native American poet. Born and raised in Nevada, he has published eight books of poetry and several novels. His first novel, *Skins*, became an award-winning movie in 2002. In 1999 he was elected to the Nevada Writers' Hall of Fame. He currently teaches at Southwest State University in Marshall, Minnesota.

Shoshone flute made from wood, metal, pitch, hide, and thread

Illustrations of Native musicians

Chapter II:

WHERE THEY CAME FROM

Scientists believe that Native Americans descended from Asian people who walked across land or ice bridges beginning perhaps 30,000 years ago. It is also possible that some came by boat. A land **migration** would have occurred at the Bering Strait, a narrow waterway between Siberia (a part of Russia) and the present state of Alaska. Sea levels might have been lower then, exposing land.

◄ BERING STRAIT

Early on Natives developed the practice of using the hide of hunted animals as clothing.

Within a few thousand years, descendants of these **immigrants** had spread across North, Central, and South America. They divided into hundreds of different groups, speaking many languages. There is evidence that in some areas they hunted huge **mammoths** and other great animals that are now extinct. Some groups wandered great distances in search of food. If water was plentiful and they could grow food, they settled down. People called the Fremont lived in the Great Basin before the Ute, Paiute, and Shoshone appeared there, probably about 1000 B.C.

Washo man etching a petroglyph

Native people adapted very well to their environment. They used the natural materials around them to make tools and clothing, to feed themselves, and to build shelters. Because of the sparse vegetation, early Great Basin residents built brush houses. Later, tribes that adopted the horse from the Plains People could travel further and hunt large animals such as elk and bison. They began to make **tipis** and to wear clothing made from skins.

Three Ute men in front of canvas-covered tipi. One has a rifle and war headdress.

What Do the Great Basin People Believe About How They Came to America?

An aged Paviotso elder from Pyramid Lake

Native People have their own stories about how they originated. Most North American tribes believed that the first parents came either from underground or from the sky. The early Great Basin People had to spend almost every waking moment searching for food, so they had less time than other Natives to tell stories. Nevertheless, a few stories survive that show an attempt to explain how people and everything else on Earth came to exist.

A Ute legend says that Pokoh, Old Man, created the world. Rainbow, Pokoh's sister, has flowers covering her breasts. Lightning strikes the ground and creates fire by filling the flint with fire. Some say the beaver brought fire from the east, hauling it on his broad, flat tail. That is why the beaver's tail has no hair on it, even to this day. It was burned off.

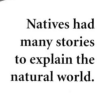

Natives had many stories to explain the natural world.

There are many worlds. Some have passed and some are still to come. In one world the Indians all creep, in another they all walk, and in another they all fly. Perhaps in a world to come, Indians may walk on four legs, crawl like snakes, or swim in the water like fish.

Pokoh created every tribe of Indians out of the soil where they used to live. That is why an Indian wants to live and die in his native place. He was made of the same soil. Pokoh did not wish men to wander and travel, but to remain in their birthplace.

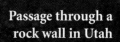

Passage through a rock wall in Utah

Coyote on the hunt

An important figure in the beliefs of the people of this region is Coyote. A story from the Paiute tells how Coyote made the world.

Coyote left his home in the Americas and traveled east across the ocean in the direction of the rising sun. In distant lands he acquired a bride and they had many children. These children were Indians, the forefathers of the great tribes that were to inhabit the North and South American continents. Preparing to return home, Coyote put them in a **wosa**, a woven willow basket jug with a stopper. Before his journey he was told not to open the wosa until he reached his country in the Great Basin.

Carved coyote

But Coyote was sly and curious. When he heard singing and the beating of **drums** from the wosa, he thought it would not hurt to take a peek. He opened the wosa. The children inside jumped out and scattered in all directions across North and South America. By the time he got the stopper back, only the Shoshone and the Paiute were left. When Coyote reached the Great Basin, he removed the stopper of the wosa and out fell the last two children.

They at once began to fight, but Coyote said to them, "You two are my children. Even though the rest got away, you two will be able to fight against the best." Thus the Shoshone and the Paiutes, who call themselves the **Newe** and **Numa** peoples, began as allies and populated the Great Basin.

(Above) illustration of Coyote. (Left) wosa made of woven willow and inside coated with tree sap

Elk and bison were hunted by Ute and Shoshone tribes that traveled great distances.

Chapter III:
LIFE IN THE GREAT BASIN

*B*efore some tribes obtained horses, many Great Basin people lived in simple **wikiups** made of brush over a hole dug in the ground. Later, the Ute and Eastern Shoshone became skilled horsemen and traveled much greater distances than before. They hunted and ate bison and elk and adopted the Plains Peoples' use of tipis made of animal skins stretched over poles. When they moved camp, the tipis were taken apart and packed onto horses.

(Above and right) examples of wikiups

Tipis were built of long poles inside and
covered with animal skin.

Pine nuts had to be gathered and shelled and were an abundant source of protein.

The Paiute and others continued what was mostly a **gathering** culture. They carried digging sticks to use in harvesting edible roots from underground. They ate the seeds of wild grasses, berries, and pine nuts. They hunted what sparse game they could find–prairie dogs, rabbits, gophers, squirrels, even mice and lizards–killing them with a **throwing-stick** or club. Occasionally, they would be able to kill an antelope. Hunters caught birds and rabbits by driving them into large nets made of woven grasses. Rabbits provided fur and leather for clothing and shelter, as well as food. In addition, people ate fish from lakes and streams, as well as roasted grasshoppers. The Mono People also ate **kuzavi**, the larva of a small fly that bred on a salty lake. They mixed it into a thick soup made of ground pine nuts.

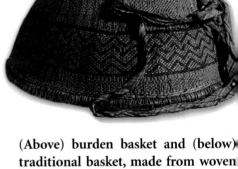

(Above) burden basket and (below) traditional basket, made from woven willow or grass

(Left) skirt made of woven grass and (below) rabbit hunting stick

Clothing was made of grass or shredded bark, crudely stitched together. For the winter, rabbit skins were woven into robes. Great Basin peoples decorated their clothing to some extent, but they did not develop the beautiful decorations found in other regions. However, some peoples such as the Shoshone and Southern Paiute became expert basket-makers. Food was cooked in baskets by first pouring water in, then dropping hot rocks into the basket until the water boiled. Women made **cradle-boards** for carrying infants out of willows and basketry. They used **burden baskets**, attached to the head and chest, to bring back pine nuts and other food items.

Cradle-board made of willow and leather

Ute garment made of hide and sinew

Arrows and quiver made by the Shoshone tribe would have been used for hunting.

Snowshoes made of wood and sinew allowed natives to track game in deep snow.

The Great Basin tribes that did not adopt the horse continued to live in this bleak region because they were relatively few, weak, and poor. Tribes that lived in the harshest climates often had to make difficult choices. For example, sick infants and elderly people sometimes could not keep up when the band moved on. They had to be left behind with a blanket and perhaps a little food that would help them last awhile.

The prosperity of some Great Basin tribes gave them the means to hunt larger game. They were also able to barter with Europeans for beads, metal, and other materials brought to the Americas.

But the Ute and Eastern Shoshone were more prosperous. They traveled into the Plains, where larger game could be hunted. They used bows and arrows more than other Great Basin groups. They stalked elk on foot in the winter, using snowshoes made from wood, leather, and plant fibers. Their clothing was of animal skins, including deer, often fringed and decorated with beads. The beads came from trading with Europeans.

Paiute beaded belt

When Europeans came, they introduced several things that had a profound influence on Native peoples–the rifle, Christianity, and contagious diseases. When Natives used rifles instead of clubs or bows and arrows to settle quarrels, the results were much more serious. Catholic and Protestant **missionaries** brought Christianity to Native peoples, teaching them that their ancient ways of living and believing were wrong. Chapter IV tells more about the Great Basin Peoples' beliefs and how their lives and beliefs are intertwined.

The worst thing Europeans brought was disease. Native people had no immunity to new diseases such as smallpox and measles, and thousands became ill and died. When Europeans first came to trade, their diseases nearly wiped some tribes out of existence.

Paiute family in Paradise Valley, Nevada, 1910

Fishing with a gaff hook
at Walker Lake

Some Great Basin Tribes

The Western Shoshone ranged from Death Valley, California, into the highlands of central Nevada and northwestern Utah. They included the Panamint of California and the Gosiute of western Utah. Pine nuts were an important food. Today, their descendants live on or near a dozen reservations in Utah, California, and Nevada. Only about 500 Gosiute, who occupied a vast area in northern Nevada and Utah, survive today.

Chiefs from Fort McDermitt Indian Reservation:
Tendoy, Skeedattle Charlie, and Little Johnnie
in Paradise Valley, Nevada, 1910

The Northern Shoshone occupied the Snake River Valley in Idaho and areas to the north. They fished for salmon, collected wild roots and vegetables, and hunted game. They acquired horses in the late 17th century and began to trade with the Crow and other tribes. They hunted bison on the Montana plains. About 3,500 Shoshone and Bannock (originally a Northern Paiute tribe) live on or near the Fort Hall Reservation in southeast Idaho. These groups hold an annual festival in August.

Pink salmon

The Eastern or Wind River Shoshone may have come from a tribe known as "Snakes" in Canada. But since about AD 1500, they have occupied parts of western Wyoming. The Comanche (a Plains tribe) separated from them in the 18th century. The Eastern Shoshone were good buffalo hunters, had tipis and horses, and observed the Plains rituals. Their chief, Washakie, helped them stay on good terms with Europeans during the 19th century. But his cooperative attitude backfired. The government forced the Shoshone to share the Wind River Reservation in Wyoming with their former enemies, the Northern Arapaho. About 2,500 Eastern Shoshone now live there.

The Ute lived in western Colorado and eastern Utah between the Green and Colorado River basins. The eastern and southern bands hunted bison, but they also gathered berries, nuts, seeds, and roots. In 1675, they made a peace treaty with the Spaniards who occupied northern New Mexico. They began trading slaves, animal hides, deer meat, and pine nuts for woven cloth, metal cooking pots, and knives.

Green River, Utah

In 1848, miners, ranchers, and settlers began pouring into Ute territory. An unpopular Indian agent, Nathan Meeker, brought on a Native rebellion. Trying to preserve their treaty rights, the Ute killed Meeker, his family, and 14 soldiers. Ute Chief Ouray, who had tried unsuccessfully to keep the peace, said, "The agreement an Indian makes to a United States treaty is like the agreement a buffalo makes with his hunters when pierced with arrows. All he can do is lie down and give in."

The Ute raided Paiute tribes, as well as Pueblo and Plains People and Mexican settlers. In turn, they were raided by Apache, Arapaho, and Cheyenne tribes. After the Meeker Massacre, the Ute were moved to the Uintah Reservation in Utah. Other tribes were moved to the Southern Ute Agency in southern Colorado, now known as the Ute Mountain and Southern Ute Reservations. About 6,400 Ute descendants live on these reservations. Thousands more have merged with the general population. The Ute Mountain Casino employs more than 380 people.

Painting depicting Josephine Meeker, wife of Nathan Meeker, on horseback with a group in native dress

Portrait of Chief Nick-A-A-God (Green Leaf). Called Ute Jack, he was involved in the Meeker Massacre.

The Paiute were composed of Southern, Eastern, and Western tribes, and also the Mono of eastern California. Perhaps 12,000 remain. The Southern Paiute were in southern Utah, Nevada, and Arizona. A related band, the Chemehuevi, lived in San Bernardino County, California. The Paiute kept on the move, seeking small game, grasshoppers, gophers, fish, and nuts and seeds to eat. They made fine baskets. Today, some have merged into the Paiute Indian Tribe of Utah, and others live on reservations in Arizona and Nevada.

The Western Mono or Monache lived along mountain rivers and shared cultural traits with some California tribes. They built houses out of bark. They now live at the Tule River Reservation and other locations nearby.

Western shore of Walker Lake

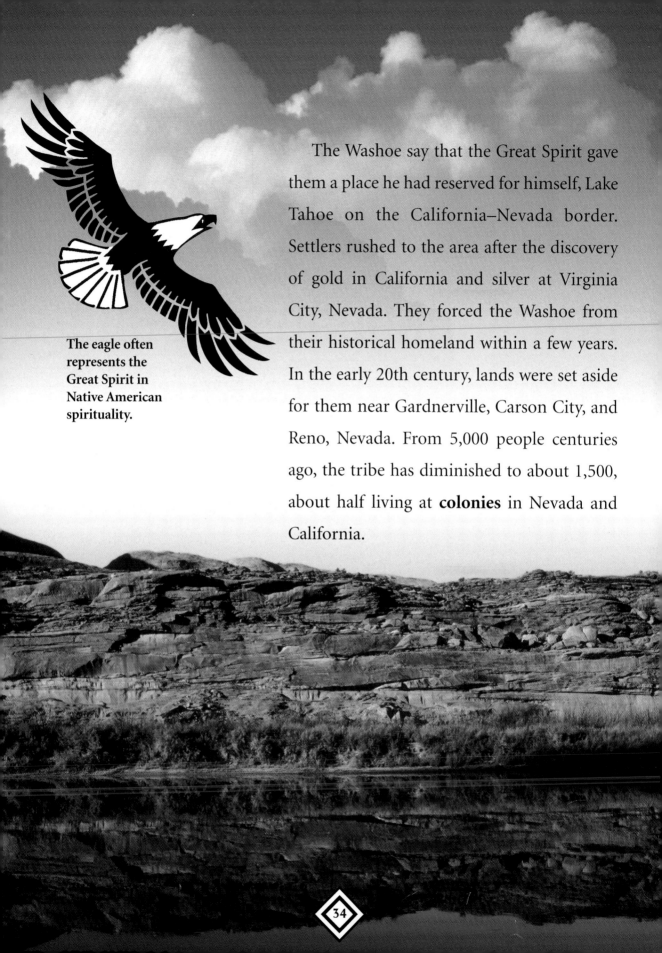

The eagle often represents the Great Spirit in Native American spirituality.

The Washoe say that the Great Spirit gave them a place he had reserved for himself, Lake Tahoe on the California–Nevada border. Settlers rushed to the area after the discovery of gold in California and silver at Virginia City, Nevada. They forced the Washoe from their historical homeland within a few years. In the early 20th century, lands were set aside for them near Gardnerville, Carson City, and Reno, Nevada. From 5,000 people centuries ago, the tribe has diminished to about 1,500, about half living at **colonies** in Nevada and California.

Chapter IV

WHAT THEY BELIEVE

*A*ll Native peoples' calendars, religion, and legends are based on nature. Their lives once depended entirely upon the earth and all that grew on it. To them, everything on Earth has a spiritual purpose and everything is interconnected. Although they may have adapted to new ways and new religions, the old faith remains alive. Their belief that nature is sacred is evident in their teachings, writings, art, and culture. It is passed from generation to generation through stories and ceremonies.

Because of their constant struggle to survive, the Great Basin People did not develop complex religions. They respected all living things and gave thanks to the spirit world for a successful hunting or gathering expedition. They did not encourage their young members to engage in **vision quests**, as the Plateau and Plains tribes did. Some men and women became **shamans,** or healers, through dreaming. They had rituals for cremating or burying their dead.

Ute medicine bag

Male elder of the Mono tribe

Dances began as ways to tell the story of a hunt or battle. The annual Bear Dance represented a chance for young men and women to find marriage partners. It lasted for up to 10 days. Many tribes also observed the **Sun Dance** and continue to dance it today. The Sun Dance is a quest for both personal spiritual power and community welfare. The dancer must first dream about being commanded to dance. Through singing and drumming, the group supports his dance. As the dancer communicates with the Great Spirit while dancing, he is aware that any "**medicine power**" he receives should be used to support the community.

Sun dancers gaze at the sun for days while dancing in place and experience visions.

The **Ghost Dance** began in the late 1800s, as a result of a vision experienced by a Paiute shaman named Wovoka. Another Paiute shaman, Wodziwob, had a similar proclamation a few years before, after the transcontinental railroad had been completed. In his vision, Woziwob saw a train arriving to bring his tribesmen back from the dead. The Paiute were to prepare themselves by reviving a Round Dance, symbolizing the sun's journey. But instead of the expected train, a drought came, which made life worse for the Paiute.

Wovoka

Painting of Ghost Dance society

Wovoka dreamed God had given him a dance to save his people. A flood would wipe out all Europeans. The spirits of Indians, dead and alive, would fly above, aided by magic feathers. To prepare for this, Natives had to practice the Ghost Dance. Soon Natives across America were dancing it. On the Great Plains, where the government had opened the sacred Black Hills to gold mining, this dance turned deadly. The belief that Natives could not be killed while dancing led to the death of an important chief, Sitting Bull, and also to a massacre at a place called Wounded Knee. The Ghost Dance died out in the early 1890s.

These visions and efforts show how desperately the Paiute and other Native People wanted to return to the time before the Europeans, when life for them was in harmony with the universe.

Drums and drumming symbolize the pulse of the universe. Drums are played during some ceremonies. Each drum is considered a sacred object and has a drum-keeper to protect it from casual use.

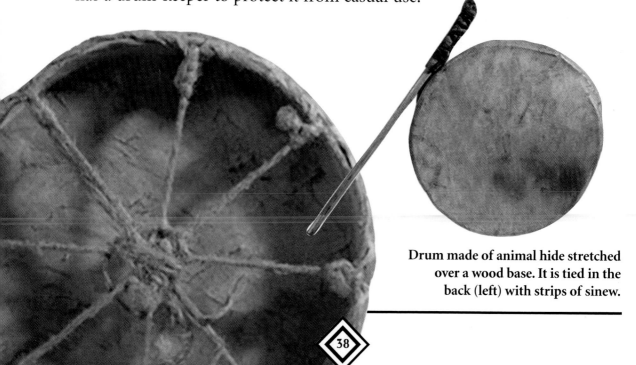

Drum made of animal hide stretched over a wood base. It is tied in the back (left) with strips of sinew.

Holding powwows is an ancient tradition among Native peoples. Though in some cultures the powwow was a religious event, today it is more of a social occasion. However, ceremonies and other religious observances may also be part of the powwow, which includes dancing, singing, feasting, and honoring old friendships.

Ute war bonnet

(Left) buffalo dancer headdress and (above) buffalo dancer illustration

Paiute tribe performing a
ceremonial dance, 1873

Many Great Basin People belong to the Native American Church. This religion involves the ritual use of **peyote**. It originated in Mexico and spread to the Plains People. Peyote is a small cactus, and people chew the center bud or use it to make tea. Today, the Native American Church of North America has 80 chapters. Worshipers sing, drum, pray, meditate, and consume peyote. Most meetings are held for healing, baptism, funerals, or birthdays.

Early Native peoples did not understand the European view that the earth is something that can be bought and sold. When European-Americans slaughtered the bison from trains or horses, just for entertainment, and left them to rot, Natives watched with astonishment. When settlers cut down forests for houses, plowed up the earth to plant crops, and fenced off the land to keep others out, Natives were shocked. Many Natives today speak of this difference in beliefs. Wovoka, the Paiute shaman, said:

"You ask me to plow the ground. Shall I take a knife and tear my mother's bosom? Then when I die she will not take me to her bosom to rest."

Farmers working

Present-day father and son

(Left) Washo man scraping a deerskin with a scraper made from an elk bone (below)

Today, many Native people are committed to healing the damage that civilization has caused to the natural environment. But in some cases, the United States has put weapons testing sites and waste disposal facilities in the sparsely populated deserts of the West. Unfortunately, these areas are frequently close to Indian reservations. In these cases, tribes try to work with state and federal government agencies to solve the environmental problems in their backyards.

Once, the survival of Native tribes depended on having strong and brave warriors, so warriors' deeds were honored through ceremonies. Today, that feeling is kept alive in the respect shown to veterans of U.S. wars. Large numbers of Native men and women have served in the Armed Forces. Native Americans have fought for the United States in every war. Veterans are honored for their willingness to die for their country. Today, powwows and tribal ceremonies often include flag songs and similar observances for Native veterans.

Portrait of Chief Winnemucca

Painting on leather hide of the wolf dance

A TIMELINE OF THE HISTORY OF
THE GREAT BASIN PEOPLE

30,000 to 13,000 BC - Ice ages lower sea levels, making it possible for people to walk across a land bridge from Asia to North America.

12,000 to 9,000 BC - Earth warms up and the ice caps melt, allowing people to move throughout North, Central, and South America.

8,000 to 1,000 BC - The Fremont, a major ancient civilization, inhabits the Great Basin.

1,000 BC to AD 1000 - Uto-Aztecan speaking people move northward and eastward into the region.

AD 1492 - Christopher Columbus arrives in America, near present-day Florida. Thinking he is in India, he names the inhabitants "Indians."

AD 1600 - Great Basin People begin to encounter Europeans. The Ute begin to raid Hopi villages.

AD 1637 - Spaniards, under Lusi de Rosas, Governor of New Mexico, capture about 80 "Utacs" (Ute) and force them to work in Santa Fe as slaves.

AD 1675 - The Spaniards make their first peace treaty with the Utes.

AD 1680 - The Pueblo Revolt drives the Spaniards out of the Southwest. They leave behind horses, which the Ute and other tribes acquire. The Ute begin to hunt bison.

AD 1750 - The Ute join the Spanish for protection against the Comanche.

AD 1776 - The American Revolution creates a new country, the United States of America.

AD 1803 - United States buys the Louisiana Territory from France for $15 million, doubling the size of the country.

AD 1804 to 1806 - The Lewis and Clark Expedition explores western lands from St. Louis to the mouth of the Columbia River. In November 1804, Sacagawea, a Shoshone woman, joins the expedition as their guide.

AD 1847 - Mormons settle near Great Salt Lake, beginning a major European impact on Great Basin People.

AD 1849 to 1859 - The California Gold Rush and the discovery of silver in Nevada bring thousands of settlers into the Great Basin.

AD 1861 to 1865 - The American Civil War is fought and ends with the abolition of slavery.

AD 1862 - The Homestead Act promises farmers free land for cultivation in the thinly populated central United States.

AD 1863 to 1868 - Shoshone resistance to settlement is broken when the U.S. Army has a major victory over the Northern Shoshone. The Eastern Shoshone of Wyoming, led by Chief Washakie, ask for a reservation at Wind River.

AD 1869 - The first transcontinental railroad is finished.

AD 1878 to 1882 - The Meeker Massacre spells the end of freedom for the Ute. Two reservations are established and they are forced to relocate.

AD 1887 - The Dawes Act allots all tribal lands in the United States to individual Natives in small parcels. Left-over parcels could be sold to non-Natives.

AD 1888 - A Paiute shaman, Wovoka, has a vision that results in the Ghost Dance, which is taken up by Plains People and other Natives across the country.

GLOSSARY

American Indian - A member of the first peoples of North America.

Aztec - The people that founded the Mexican empire conquered by Cortes in 1519.

Bear Dance - A favorite dance of the Ute and other tribes. Part of the spring celebration, in which young people looked for mates.

burden basket - A basket made to sling over the back or shoulders for carrying goods.

camp - Temporary living space for a band of 50 to 200 Great Basin People.

casino - A building used for gambling.

colony - Small reservations, mainly in Nevada and California.

cradle-board - A woven or sewn pouch attached to a stiffer frame made of wood or reeds for holding an infant securely.

drum - A hollow instrument with coverings, such as skins, over the ends, which can be beaten to make a rhythmic sound.

drumming - Making a series of strokes or vibrations that produce rhythmic sounds.

gathering - Collecting food or raw materials from the wild; also, a meeting.

Ghost Dance - One of several dances originating among the Paiute, which were performed to bring back the spirits of the dead and the prosperity of Native people.

Great Basin People - The Natives of a region defined as having cultural and environmental similarities, now made up of Utah, Nevada, and parts of adjacent states.

immigrant - A person who comes to a country to live in it.

kuzavi - Mono word for the edible fly larva from a salty lake.

Lewis and Clark Expedition - Exploration of the Louisiana Purchase and the country beyond by Meriwether Lewis and William Clark to find a land route to the Pacific Ocean.

mammoth - Extinct hairy elephants living about 1,600,000 years ago.

medicine power - The power received from the Great Spirit while dancing the Sun Dance.

migration - The movement of a person or group from one country or place to another.

missionary - A person who goes on an assignment to convert people to that person's beliefs or religion.

Mormon - A church founded in New York in 1830 by Joseph Smith, now called The Reorganized Church of Jesus Christ of Latter-day Saints. A member of that church.

Native American - A synonym for American Indian. Some Natives prefer it because it eliminates the mistaken term "Indian." Other Natives prefer the old term.

Newe - Shoshone word for themselves.

Numa - Paiute word for themselves.

Oregon Trail - Route from Independence, Missouri, to the Columbia River region.

peyote - A small cactus (also called "mescal") or its center bud.

powwow - Originally referred to a shaman, a vision, or a gathering. Now, it means a cultural, social, and spiritual gathering to celebrate Native culture and pride.

reservation - A tract of public land set aside for a specific use. Tracts set aside for Natives. In Canada, they are called "reserves."

Sacagawea - The Shoshone woman who guided and interpreted during the Lewis and Clark Expedition.

semiarid - Having about 10 to 20 inches (25 to 51 cm) of rainfall a year.

shaman - Medicine man or woman.

Shoshonean - Relating to a large, extensive language family, also called Uto-Aztecan.

sinew - Fiber from tendons, the animal tissue that connects muscles. Sinew was used as thread and for other purposes.

sinkhole - A hollow place or depression that collects water from rain or drainage.

sovereign nation - A community of people that has independent power and freedom from outside control.

Sun Dance - A major religious ceremony of most Native tribes west of the Missouri River in the early 1800s.

throwing-stick - A wooden pole or stick with a stone spearhead, a more primitive tool for hunting than a bow and arrows.

tipi - A conical tent made of poles and skins, which can be packed up and moved from place to place.

treaty An agreement or arrangement, usually written, made by negotiating.

Uto-Aztecan - A major language family of the Southwest, also known as Shoshonean.

vision quest - A perception that a young Native seeks when going on a "vision quest," which will guide him or her through life.

wikiup - Hut built of sticks or canes for a frame and brush, grass, or bark for a covering.

wosa - Paiute word for a woven willow basket jug with a stopper.

Books of Interest

Erlich, Amy, adapter. *Wounded Knee: An Indian History of the American West.* New York: Henry Holt & Co. 1993 (adaptation for young readers of Dee Brown's *Bury My Heart at Wounded Knee,* Henry Holt & Co., 1970).

Erdoes, Richard and Alfonso Ortiz, eds. *American Indian Myths and Legends.* New York: Pantheon, 1984.

Franklin, Robert J. and Pamela A Bunte. *The Paiute.* New York: Chelsea House Publishers, 1990.

Johnson, Michael. *Encyclopedia of Native Tribes of North America.* New York: Gramercy Books, 2001.

La Farge, Oliver. *The American Indian.* New York: Golden Press, 1956.

Nerburn, Kent, ed. *The Wisdom of the Native Americans.* Novato, Calif.: New World Library, 1999.

Sherrow, Victoria. *Indians of the Plateau and Great Basin.* New York: Facts On File, 1992.

Thomasma, Kenneth and Eunice Hundley. *Shoshoni Girl Who Ran.* Jackson, Wyoming: Grandview Publishing Company, 1983.

Woodhead, Henry, series ed. *The American Indians.* Alexandria, Va.: Time Life Inc., 1992-94.

Children's Atlas of Native Americans. Chicago: Rand McNally & Co., 1996.

Good Web Sites to Begin Researching Native Americans

General Information Site with Links
http://www.nativeculture.com

Resources for Indigenous Cultures around the World
http://www.nativeweb.org/

Index of Native American Resources on the Internet
http://www.hanksville.org/NAresources/

News and Information from a Native American Perspective
http://www.indianz.com

An Online Newsletter Celebrating Native America
http://www.turtletrack.org

Native American History in the United States
http://web.uccs.edu/~history/index/nativeam.html

Internet School Library Media Center
http://falcon.jmu.edu/~ramseyil/native.htm

INDEX

Linda Thompson is a Montana native and a graduate of the University of Washington. She has been a teacher, writer, and editor in the San Francisco Bay Area for 30 years and now lives in Taos, New Mexico. She can be contacted through her web site, http://www.highmesaproductions.com